Who Is
Dale Earnhardt Jr.?

by David Stabler

illustrated by Dede Putra

Penguin Workshop

PENGUIN WORKSHOP
An imprint of Penguin Random House LLC, New York

First published in the United States of America by Penguin Workshop,
an imprint of Penguin Random House LLC, New York, 2022

Visit us online at penguinrandomhouse.com.

Library of Congress Cataloging-in-Publication Data is available.

Printed in the United States of America

ISBN 9780593225967 (paperback)   10 9 8 7 6 5 4 3 2 1 WOR
ISBN 9780593225974 (library binding)   10 9 8 7 6 5 4 3 2 1 WOR

Contents

Who Is Dale Earnhardt Jr.?

"Gentlemen, start your engines!"

With those four words, the 2004 Daytona 500 was underway. The five-hundred-mile auto race is one of the biggest events in sports, attracting drivers from all over the world. Among those revving their motors at the starting grid was twenty-nine-year-old Dale Earnhardt Jr., one of the most popular drivers in NASCAR.

Dale had never won the Daytona 500. But he had an extra-special reason to want to win this one. Exactly six years earlier, on February 15, 1998, Dale's father had won *his* first Daytona 500 on this very track. Now it was "Junior's" turn.

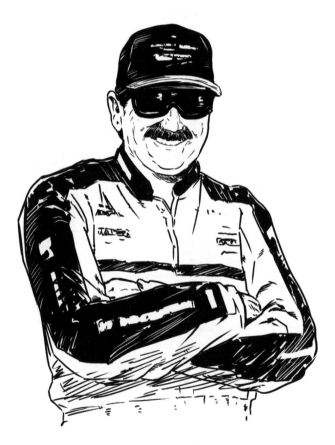

Dale Earnhardt Sr.

Dale even had the date stamped on the hood of his car to inspire him to victory: 15 FEB 2004.

After a few practice laps to get the cars revved up and ready, actress Whoopi Goldberg dropped the green flag—and the race was on!

From the start, it was a close one. Dale took the early lead, his white car emblazoned with a red #8 zipping around the track. A crowd of nearly two hundred thousand cheered him on through every tight turn. But the other drivers would not let up the chase. They had victory on their minds as well. Jeff Gordon surged into the lead at one point. Then Tony Stewart passed them both. It was going to be a fight to the finish.

With just under thirty laps to go, Dale decided it was time to make his move. For the next eight trips around the track, he tried every trick he knew to edge Tony Stewart out of the top spot. But Stewart blocked him every time.

At last, Dale saw an opening. He dropped back behind Stewart, sneaked around the side, then gunned his engine. In one burst, #8 surged to the head of the pack.

With only a few laps to go, all Dale had to do was hold on to his lead. Tony Stewart did all

he could to keep up, but Junior kept him from pulling ahead. He crossed the finish line, taking first place by less than one second. The winner's trophy—and a prize of more than $1 million— belonged to him.

After the race, Dale headed to a special part of the track called Victory Lane to celebrate with the fans. Along the way, he leaned out of the driver's side window, punching his fist in the air and whooping with joy. "This has got to be the greatest day of my life!" he told the cheering crowd. It was his fifth try at winning the Daytona 500. His dad had also lost there many times before finally winning the "Great American Race."

Dale was filled with pride as he left the track that afternoon. He had finally achieved his number one goal in racing. And though he was sad that his father was not there to see it, he believed that he had done his family proud. Most NASCAR fans would agree. Dale Sr. had always been a favorite with the crowds at Daytona. Now they had a new hero named Earnhardt to cheer for.

Dale Earnhardt Jr. would go on to win

many more races after that one. He was named NASCAR's Most Popular Driver fifteen years in a row—a record streak. He would even return to Victory Lane at Daytona. But that first victory may have been the sweetest of them all.

CHAPTER 1
Coming Up Fast

Dale Earnhardt Jr. was born on October 10, 1974, in Kannapolis, North Carolina. His father, Dale Earnhardt Sr., was one of NASCAR's most popular drivers. His mother, Brenda Gee Earnhardt, was the daughter of a master race car builder. So you could say Dale Jr. had racing in his blood.

When Dale was a toddler, his parents got divorced. Dale and his sister, Kelley, who was two years older than him, lived with their mom, Brenda. Three years after the divorce, their house caught on fire and burned to the ground. Fortunately, no one was hurt. With no place to go, Brenda moved to Norfolk, Virginia, to stay with her own mother. Dale and Kelley stayed behind in North Carolina and moved in with their dad. Their mom remained close to them and would often come back to visit.

Dale Earnhardt Jr. and mother, Brenda

It was fun having a NASCAR star for a father. On race days, Dale would sit on the living room carpet playing with Matchbox cars while listening to the radio broadcast of his dad's race. He and Kelley also liked to watch Dale Sr. work on his cars in the garage.

But the busy life of a NASCAR driver was hard on the family as well. From February to November, Dale Sr. raced almost every weekend in a different town. He could afford to pay babysitters, nannies, and housekeepers to look after Dale Jr. and Kelley, but he was often away from home.

Their father may not have been around a lot, but Kelley was always there for Dale.

She became like a second mom to her little brother. At school, she gave him lunch money and tried to keep him out of trouble on the playground. Because Dale was smaller than other kids his age, he got picked on a lot. Kelley made sure to protect him from bullies.

Like a lot of children who are bullied, Dale began to act out in school—and at home. One time, he came upon a glass bottle full of coins in

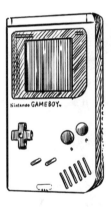

his father's bedroom. He pulled the antenna off his father's car, stuck some tape to the end of it, and fished more than eighty dollars worth of quarters out of the bottle. He used the money to buy a Game Boy.

When the housekeeper discovered what Dale had done, she told his father. Dale Sr. had locks put on every door of the house. Then he hid the keys so Junior couldn't raid any more change jars.

Clearly, Dale needed something constructive to do with his time and energy. When he was twelve, he started racing go-karts on the streets. But he crashed so many times his father ordered him to stop.

At school, Dale continued pulling pranks and getting into fights with other boys. Even Kelley couldn't keep him out of trouble anymore. Dale Sr. began to worry that Dale might fail school and have to leave. After thinking about it for a long time, he decided to send Dale away to a military school. Kelley still wanted to keep an eye on her little brother, so she went with him and enrolled there, too.

Oak Ridge Military Academy was very different from the public school Dale had left behind. Students at Oak Ridge had to wake up every morning at 6:30 and did not get to go to bed until the bugle sounded at 10:00 at night. Before breakfast, Dale had to shine his shoes and polish the brass buttons on his uniform.

He ate all his meals in a large "mess hall" and had to study for two hours at his desk every night from Sunday through Thursday. The only time he got to spend alone, without someone watching over him, was from 3:00 p.m. to 6:00 p.m. each day. Worst of all, if he broke any of the school rules, he was not allowed to go home on the weekend.

Dale made sure to follow all the rules and stay out of trouble. He stopped misbehaving in class and started getting better grades. After a year and a half at Oak Ridge, it was time for him to move on. He returned home and began his freshman year at Mooresville High School.

Though life at military school was difficult, Dale learned a lot. He believed that his time at Oak Ridge had made him a better person. Now he needed a new challenge. And if he thought he was going to have it easy at Mooresville High, he was wrong.

CHAPTER 2
Off to the Races

Dale had a hard time fitting in at his new school. He wasn't considered one of the "cool kids" and had difficulty making friends. He also had trouble finding a sport that was right for him. Because he was too small for football, he played soccer his freshman year. But he was not very

good at it. He often dreamed about being behind the wheel of a race car, like his father.

When he turned sixteen in 1990, Dale got his driver's license. This was his big chance. He sold one of his old go-karts for $500. Then he headed down to the town junkyard and used the money to buy his first car—a 1978 Chevrolet Monte Carlo. It was ten years old and not in the best condition, but it was all his.

1978 Chevrolet Monte Carlo

Around that time, Dale also became friends with his half brother, Kerry, Dale Sr.'s son from a previous marriage. Kerry, who was then twenty-one, shared Dale's love of racing and offered to help him transform the Monte Carlo into a top-notch race car.

Together, Dale and Kerry spent nearly every weekend working on the car. Luckily, the Monte Carlo had no dents. The motor ran just fine. It didn't take them long to get it into tip-top shape. The boys even painted a number on its side like a real NASCAR vehicle. Now they just had to find a place to race.

Dale heard about a nearby track that was starting up a new race series for "street stock" cars—cars without any special modifications. Concord Motorsports Park allowed young

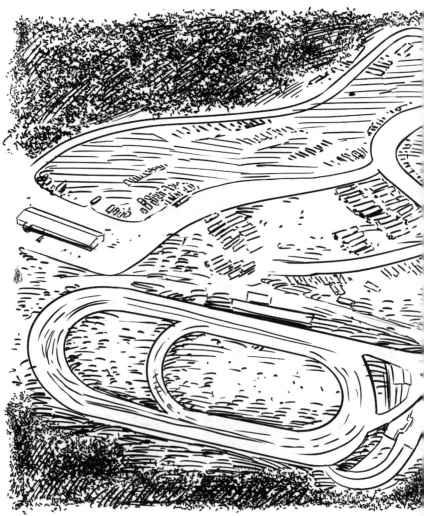

drivers to compete on a quarter-mile asphalt "short track" on weekends. It was a great way for a new racer like Dale to practice. Best of all, you got paid no matter where you finished,

Concord Motorsports Park

so even the worst drivers got to go home with some prize money.

For the next two years, Dale and Kerry took turns behind the wheel of the Monte Carlo at Motorsports Park. On weekdays, Dale continued to attend classes at Mooresville High. And every evening he'd head into the garage to try to add some new improvement to his car.

After graduating from high school, Dale enrolled in Mitchell Community College. He earned a college degree in automotive technology and worked part-time as a mechanic in his father's garage. He learned how to fix engines, change oil, and repair tires on the fly. All the while he kept racing.

Dale quickly learned that he could make more money racing cars than repairing them. Even when he came in last in a race, he still took home more prize money than he would earn in a week working in his father's garage!

Dale became convinced that he should make racing his full-time career.

The next level up after street stock is the late-model division. In 1992, the year he turned eighteen, Dale set his sights on conquering this division. He traded in the old Monte Carlo for a new car—a sleek, fast, modern race car. Now instead of just having Kerry help him keep his car in condition, Dale had a pit crew, or team, working by his side.

Dale ran his first late-model race at Myrtle Beach Speedway in South Carolina. He didn't win. In fact, it would take him nearly two years to win a race on the late-model circuit.

In all, he won only three out of the 113 races he entered. Though he didn't get to take home many trophies, Dale did finish in the top ten more often than not. Most important of all, he was gaining experience and earning the respect of his fellow drivers.

In 1996, Dale got an exciting big break. When another driver had to drop out, he was invited to fill in for him in a race in the Busch Series, NASCAR's highest minor league. Now he was just one step away from joining his father on the most challenging circuit in American racing!

Dale's first Busch Series race did not go as well as he hoped. He finished fourteenth, taking home just $1,880 in prize money. But it was a start. Afterwards, Dale's uncle Danny Earnhardt

called Dale Sr. and reported: "The boy can drive."

The next year, Dale continued to race part-time in the Busch Series. All told, he earned more than $50,000 in prize money. As 1998 dawned, Dale felt like he was climbing his way to the top ranks of NASCAR. The race was on—and he was just getting revved up.

The Story of NASCAR

 William "Bill" France Sr. (1909–1992) was a gas station owner from Washington, DC. He loved cars and was fascinated by the idea of making them run faster. He heard about a track in Daytona Beach, Florida, where drivers were setting land speed records.

In the spring of 1935, France moved to Daytona Beach, where he opened up an auto repair shop. He quickly made friends with other drivers and racing fans who came into his shop. He even started racing cars and promoting races himself.

After seeing how big the crowds were at these events, France gathered a group of car owners and drivers together to form the National Association for Stock Car Racing—or NASCAR. The number one rule of the new organization was that drivers must race "stock" cars—ordinary vehicles that were not souped-up, or modified, in any way. France was named NASCAR's first president.

The first official NASCAR race was held on June 19, 1949, at the Charlotte Speedway in North Carolina. More than thirteen thousand fans showed up to watch thirty-three drivers compete in the 150-mile, 200-lap race.

Today, more than a hundred thousand show up to a typical NASCAR event—a tribute to the influence of Big Bill on the sport of racing.

The Road to NASCAR

To make it in NASCAR, a driver must climb the ranks. Just as baseball players progress through various minor leagues on their way to the major leagues, stock car drivers gain experience in three local racing "circuits" before they make it to NASCAR races.

STREET STOCK

The street stock circuit is for drivers who are just starting out. Drivers on this circuit drive cars with engines that are unmodified, as if they had just been bought out of an auto dealer's stock.

SUPER STOCK

Super stock is a higher level of street stock. On this circuit, drivers are allowed to modify, or soup up, their engines. Due to their high horsepower and relatively light weight, it is not uncommon for super stock cars to perform big wheelies off the starting line.

Super stock car

LATE MODEL

On the late-model circuit, drivers are allowed to make even more modifications to their engines. Some late-model cars are even custom built. Because of the time and money needed to make these modifications, most drivers take several years to reach the late-model circuit.

AND FINALLY . . . NASCAR

Not so fast. Before a driver can make it onto the main NASCAR circuit, they must first compete in the NASCAR Xfinity Series, NASCAR's official "minor league" circuit. This used to be known as the Busch Series. Xfinity Series drivers run their races on Saturdays, while top NASCAR Cup Series drivers run on Sundays.

CHAPTER 3
Like Father, Like Son

The 1998 Daytona 500 was run on a gray, cool Sunday afternoon in Daytona Beach on the east coast of Florida. The weekend did not go well for Dale Earnhardt Jr. He crashed his car during his Busch Series race on Saturday. Fortunately, he was not badly hurt. But he decided to go home early to rest and recover. Unfortunately,

that meant he would not be around to see his father's greatest victory at the Daytona International Speedway.

By 1998, Dale Earnhardt Sr. had almost given up on his chances of winning the Daytona 500. He had run the race nineteen times. Each time he had lost. This time, however, luck was on his side.

On the day before the big race, a little girl in a wheelchair approached Dale Sr. after practice. She handed him a penny and said, "I rubbed this penny and it's going to win you the Daytona 500." The fearsome driver known as "the Intimidator" smiled and glued the coin to the dashboard of his car.

The next day, Dale Sr. roared to victory in the Great American Race. Throngs of cheering fans greeted him in Victory Lane as he raised his fists in triumph. Right then and there, he vowed to keep the "lucky penny" glued to his dashboard forever.

The Great American Race

The Daytona 500, known as the Great American Race, has been run every year since 1959. But its roots go all the way back to 1903. That was the year two men on Ormand Beach, just north of Daytona, Florida, got into an argument over which one of them had the fastest "horseless carriage." They settled their dispute by running a race across the sand.

The race drew a crowd. Soon, other beachgoers joined in the fun. Daytona Beach became known as the "Birthplace of Speed." Racing in Daytona became so popular that NASCAR founder Bill France organized the construction of a 2.5-mile "superspeedway." Daytona International Speedway took more than a year to build and opened in 1959.

That February, the first Daytona 500 was run. The race was so close, it took three days to figure out that driver Lee Petty had won. That was just the first of many fantastic finishes at the track known as the "World Center of Racing."

Dale was disappointed to have missed his father's big win. He had to wait to give his congratulations back home in North Carolina. But there would be more days of celebration ahead for the Earnhardts in 1998.

In April of that year, Dale won his first Busch Series race at Texas Motor Speedway. His dad was there to cheer on his victory. In fact, Dale Sr. was scheduled to race on the same track the

very next day. With half brother Kerry also making a name for himself on the minor league circuit, the Earnhardts were now considered to be the "First Family" of NASCAR.

The rest of 1998 was a blur—which is what the other drivers usually saw when Dale sped past them on the track.

Dale racked up six more Busch Series wins, taking home more than a million dollars in prize money. At the end of the year, he was named 1998 Busch Series champion. But he wasn't about to stop there.

The following year, Junior took his racing to the next level—in more ways than one. At age twenty-five, he continued to dominate the Busch Series, upping his yearly winnings to more than $1.6 million and taking home his second straight series crown. But he had his eye on the top NASCAR circuit. "I want to race on Sunday," Dale declared. On May 30, 1999, he got his chance.

Dale had done so well in the Busch Series that he was promoted to the "major leagues" of NASCAR. A crowd of 128,000 gathered at Charlotte Motor Speedway to watch the race. Dale drove a fire-engine red car with #8 painted on the side in white. As he fastened his seat belt and pulled on his helmet before the start, he felt nervous, but excited.

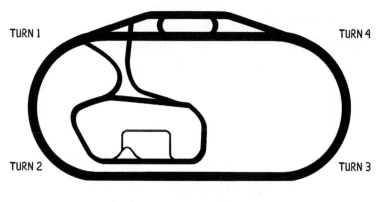

Charlotte Motor Speedway, 1999

Dale had never been in a race this long before. At six hundred miles from start to finish, it was twice as long as most Busch Series races. Dale's endurance would be tested along with his driving skills.

The length of the race wasn't the only challenge. The competition was stiffer, too. Dale was no longer racing against other minor leaguers. The forty-two drivers in this race were some of the best NASCAR had to offer. They had years of experience on him. When the starting flag was waved, it showed. Dale held his own for much of the race, but he faded at the finish and ended up in sixteenth place. Still, he had proved he belonged on the same track as some of the greatest drivers in the world.

Dale raced four more times in the 1999 NASCAR Cup Series. He never finished higher than tenth. But there was a buzz about him. Everywhere he went, he drew a crowd of fans and autograph seekers. Racing magazines began to write articles about him. Sometimes they asked Dale Sr. to pose in photographs with him.

Dale did not mind being compared to his famous father. He was happy to get some attention, and he always valued his dad's advice. But he knew that now that he had made the leap to NASCAR Cup racing, he would have to prove himself worthy of all that attention. In 2000, that's just what he did.

The NASCAR Glossary

- *Checkered flag*: the black-and-white flag waved at the end of a race
- *Green flag*: the flag that signals the start of a race
- *Oval*: slang term for a race track
- *Pit crew*: a group of people who maintain a car during a race
- *Red flag*: the flag that is waved to stop a race
- *Short track*: a track that is less than one mile long
- *Speedway*: a track that is between one and two miles long
- *Superspeedway*: a track that is more than two miles long

- *Victory Lane*: the part of the track where the winner goes to celebrate
- *Yellow flag*: a cautionary flag, telling drivers to slow down and remain in their positions until the track is safe

Start Your Engines

A stock car's engine is one of the most awesome machines ever invented. It is engineered to power a car traveling at tremendous speed for hundreds of miles.

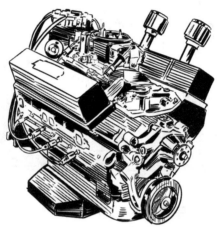

The temperature inside a NASCAR engine can reach almost three hundred degrees Fahrenheit. Top racing speeds can approach 200 miles per hour. Some cars can even go airborne if they spin sideways. In 1987, driver Bill Elliott became

NASCAR's fastest man when he went 212.8 miles per hour at Talladega Superspeedway.

To make sure drivers stay safe at top speeds, NASCAR has added a number of safety features to their cars over the years. The *restrictor plate* restricts the amount of air and fuel that can go into the engine, slowing the car down. The *roll cage* protects the driver in the event of a crash. *Roof flaps* deploy if a car spins out, to keep it from becoming airborne. And the Head and Neck Support, or *HANS Device*, keeps a driver's head stable at all times.

CHAPTER 4
Tragedy

The year 2000 was full of milestones for Dale and his family. In February, he and Dale Sr. raced against each other at the Daytona 500 for the first time. Junior finished thirteenth, eight places ahead of his father.

In April, Dale Jr. won his first NASCAR Cup race. It was only his twelfth start in the "big leagues." That broke the rookie record set by—who else?—Dale Sr.

Then, in August, not one, not two, but *three* Earnhardts lined up against one another for the Pepsi 400 at Michigan International Speedway. Dale Sr., Dale Jr., and Kerry had never competed in the same race before. In fact, it was only the second time in history that a father raced against

Dale Earnhardt Jr. (#8) and Dale Earnhardt Sr. (#3)
race against each other at the 2000 Daytona 500.

two of his sons. This time, Dale Sr. led the way.
He finished sixth, with Junior coming in thirty-
first and Kerry bringing up the rear in forty-third
place.

Dale Jr., Dale Sr., and Kerry Earnhardt

That was one of the few disappointing finishes for Dale Jr. in 2000. At year's end, because it was his first full year on the circuit, he was up for Rookie of the Year honors. While Dale was edged out by another first-year driver, Matt Kenseth, he could look back on a successful season in which he racked up two wins and five top-ten finishes.

Matt Kenseth

As 2001 dawned, it seemed like nothing could hold Dale back from another record-smashing season. Then tragedy struck.

That February's Daytona 500 gave Dale another chance to compete against his father. The Florida weather that Sunday was perfect for racing—pleasant, with temperatures in the sixties. Everyone in the crowd expected a close race.

As the drivers entered the final lap, it looked
like they were headed for a fantastic finish. Dale
Jr., Dale Sr., and Michael Waltrip were neck and
neck for first place, with Sterling Marlin closing

in fast. Then something went horribly wrong. Marlin's car bumped into Dale Sr.'s and sent him crashing head-on into the wall that ringed the track. Dale Sr. was killed instantly.

Dale Sr.'s fatal crash

Black Sunday

NASCAR legend Dale Earnhardt Sr. dies after Daytona 500 crash

Dale Jr. completed the final lap, finishing second. It was only then that he learned that the accident had taken his father's life. Dale Sr. was forty-nine years old. It was a day of terrible sadness for the Earnhardts—and NASCAR fans everywhere. The newspapers called it "Black Sunday."

In the days after his father's passing, Dale gathered together with family. Cards and letters

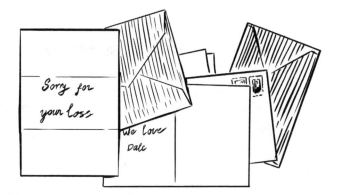

poured in from all over the country, expressing sympathy for the Earnhardts. President George W. Bush even called to offer his sympathy.

President George W. Bush

Dale Earnhardt Sr. (1951–2001)

One of the most successful drivers in NASCAR history, Dale Earnhardt Sr. was born in Kannapolis, North Carolina. He made his racing debut in 1975, at the age of twenty-four.

Fans called him "the Intimidator" because he wore dark clothes and drove with an aggressive, hard-charging style. He was also known as "Ironhead," "the Big E," and "the Man in Black." Earnhardt's black #3 Chevrolet was one of the most recognizable cars in racing.

In 1980, Earnhardt won his first NASCAR championship. He was the first driver to win Rookie of the Year and the NASCAR championship in

back-to-back seasons. He was also the first driver to top $30 million in career earnings.

Over the course of his twenty-six-year career, Dale Earnhardt Sr. racked up:

- 7 NASCAR championships
- 76 all-time wins
- 428 top-ten finishes

He was named the National Motorsports Press Association's Driver of the Year five times. He was inducted into the International Motor Sports Hall of Fame in 2006 and the NASCAR Hall of Fame in 2010.

At first, Dale did not feel like speaking to reporters. But people expected him to say *something*. They also wanted to know if he was ever going to race again. Five days after his father's death, Dale spoke at a press conference. He announced his plans to return to the track

the following weekend. "I'm sure he'd want us to keep going," he said of his dad, "and that's what we're going to do." He also urged NASCAR fans not to blame Sterling Marlin for his father's tragic accident.

The next weekend, Dale returned to the track.

But his heart just wasn't in it. He slammed into a wall on the first lap. It was a common sight at NASCAR races, but coming so soon after Dale Sr.'s crash, it put everybody on edge. Many in the crowd held their breath, fearing the worst. Dale came out okay, but he ended up finishing in forty-third place. He knew it would take some time before he could return to top form.

Dale continued to struggle on the track throughout the spring and summer of 2001. Everywhere he went he was greeted by tributes to his father. At one track, a fifty-foot-high number three was painted on the grass in Dale Sr.'s honor. These reminders of his father's death made it hard for Dale to concentrate on his own driving. Slowly but surely, however, he began to get his confidence back.

In July, Dale returned to Daytona for the first time since the accident. The superspeedway was hosting the Pepsi 400, a four-hundred-mile race. A large crowd gathered to cheer Dale on to victory.

At first, it looked like Dale might have to settle for a top-ten finish. Then the race took a turn. It took twenty-six laps, but Dale's #8 Chevrolet finally pulled into the lead. He held off a furious charge by Michael Waltrip and won the race as the crowd roared with approval.

Dale wins 2001 Pepsi 400

Entering Victory Lane, Dale pumped his fist in celebration. Asked by a reporter for his comment on the race, Dale said he was thinking of his father. "He was with me tonight," he said. "I don't know how I did it. I dedicate this win to him."

CHAPTER 5
Dalemania

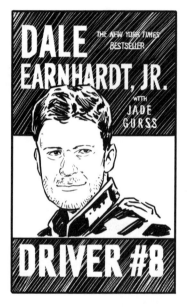

By the end of 2001, Dale was one of the most successful drivers in NASCAR.

That year, Dale wrote his first book, *Driver #8*. The book told the story of his rookie season in 2000. Some people didn't think the book would sell well. They didn't think NASCAR was popular enough, especially outside of the South.

But when it came out, *Driver #8* quickly became a best seller. In fact, it is one of the most popular racing books ever published. Even people who had never been to a NASCAR race were interested in Dale's story.

Suddenly, Dale was in demand. Magazines that had never covered racing before wanted to do stories about him. Hollywood producers called to see if he wanted to appear in television shows and movies. In the past, Dale would have said no to all these offers. He told friends he was too shy and did not want all the added attention. Just being a winning driver and pleasing his fans was enough for him. But now he was ready for the spotlight. He set out to become one of the most famous athletes in the world. Dalemania was about to begin.

Dale agreed to be shown on the cover of a NASCAR video game.

He had his car painted yellow and decorated with the logo of his sponsor, the Nilla Wafers cookie brand. And when a producer at MTV asked if he wanted to present an award at the network's annual Video Music Awards in 2001, Dale said yes. Now he just had to come up with something to wear.

On the afternoon of the awards ceremony, Dale met with a stylist who helped him pick out a leather jacket to wear that night. Then a limousine whisked him away to the event, held at New York City's Metropolitan Opera House. Dale was excited to be walking the red carpet alongside so many superstars of rock, R&B, and hip-hop.

But he was also terrified about appearing on stage in front of so many people. When the time came, he stepped up to the microphone and said his lines perfectly.

Dale grew accustomed to being famous. He acted in an episode of the TV sitcom *Yes, Dear*.

Dale acting on the set of *Yes, Dear*

Dale and Will Ferrell in *Talladega Nights*

He also appeared as a "special guest" in a number of music videos alongside Sheryl Crow, Jay-Z, Trace Adkins, Kid Rock, and Nickelback. Pop, country, rap—it didn't matter what type of music. Dale was popular with music fans everywhere. He even had a small role in the NASCAR comedy *Talladega Nights*, a movie starring Will Ferrell.

Talladega Nights

Talladega Nights is a 2006 comedy movie starring Will Ferrell as Ricky Bobby, a champion NASCAR driver. His motto is "If you ain't first, you're last."

The movie takes place at the Talladega Superspeedway in Alabama, although it was mostly filmed in North Carolina. Dale Earnhardt Jr. has a small part as himself. Several other NASCAR drivers also appear in the film.

Although *Talladega Nights* is one of the most popular NASCAR movies ever made, it wasn't the first. Here are a few others:

SPEEDWAY (1968)

King of rock 'n' roll Elvis Presley stars as stock car driver Steve Grayson. The first NASCAR musical!

GREASED LIGHTNING (1977)

Comedian Richard Pryor plays Wendell Scott, the first Black driver to win a NASCAR race.

DAYS OF THUNDER (1990)

Tom Cruise stars as rookie NASCAR driver Cole Trickle.

CARS (2006)

This Pixar cartoon follows rookie race car Lightning McQueen on his quest to win the Piston Cup.

As Dale's fame grew, so did his need for his own space. After thinking about it for a long time, he decided to move out of his family home. He had made so much money racing that he could afford his own house. He decided to build on his family's property in North Carolina.

But his was no ordinary house. Dale decked out his new home with the largest and loudest big-screen televisions, video game consoles, and a computer room. He even turned his basement into a nightclub, complete with speakers as high

as the ceiling and a dance floor.

Dale started his own racing company—a team of drivers—in 2002. He also reconnected with his mother, Brenda, when she moved back to North Carolina from Virginia. Dale began to think about settling down and starting his own family.

FONTANA

On the track, "Little E"—as he was sometimes known—continued to dominate. In 2002, he was heading toward another record-breaking season. Then, in late April, during a race in Fontana, California, the car in front of Dale's got a flat tire and veered into his. The resulting crash was one of the most violent

of Dale's racing career. A doctor later determined
that Dale had suffered a severe concussion—
a brain injury. For the next few months, Dale
had headaches and difficulty concentrating. He
went into the first slump of his racing career. It
wasn't until October that he started feeling better
again.

In 2003, Dale made a strong comeback from his injury. He finished number three in driver rankings for the year. He earned more than $6 million total in prize winnings and was voted Most Popular Driver by NASCAR fans. But the one prize he wanted most was still just out of reach. For 2004, Dale focused on winning his first Daytona 500. When he completed that task, six years to the day after his father had won his, he knew that he had truly become NASCAR's biggest superstar.

CHAPTER 6
New Beginnings

When all was said and done, Dale won the 2004 Daytona 500 by less than a second. That's how close Tony Stewart came to catching him.

Dale was on top for now, but he knew he'd have to keep working hard to stop younger, hungrier drivers from passing him by.

That July, Dale suffered one of the worst crashes of his career. During warm-ups for a race in California, he crashed into a concrete barrier and his car caught on fire. Luckily, Dale managed to climb out of the burning cockpit and scramble to safety. But he was badly burned on his neck, chin, and legs.

After healing up from his accident, Dale came back strong. He won six races and $8.9 million in prize money for the year. He was named NASCAR's Most Popular Driver for the second year in a row.

Dale followed up with strong racing seasons in 2005 and 2006 as well. By 2007, however, he felt it was time for a change.

Ever since he started racing, Dale had driven for the racing team founded by his father, Dale Earnhardt Inc., or DEI. In a way, driving for DEI helped Dale keep his dad's memory alive. But it also reminded him of how much he missed Dale Sr. Maybe it would be better, Dale thought, if he struck out on his own.

In the spring of 2007, when he was thirty-two, Dale announced that he would leave Dale Earnhardt Inc. at the end of the year to drive for a new team, Hendrick Motorsports. He also decided to give up the number 8 and switch to number 88. That was the number used by his father's father, Ralph Earnhardt, back in the 1950s.

No matter the number, Dale proved hard to catch on the NASCAR oval. Driving a new car, with a new team, he showed the same old competitive fire. He finished in the top ten in eleven of his first fifteen races in 2008, in what was considered a down year for him. But his biggest win may have come off the track.

In the fall of 2008, Dale hired an interior design company to help him make some improvements on his house. One of the designers was a young woman named Amy Reimann.

Amy Reimann

Dale liked Amy immediately and thought about asking her out on a date, but he was too shy to do so. Instead, he asked one of his close friends, T. J. Majors, to set up a meeting with the design team so that Dale would have an excuse to introduce himself to Amy.

The minute they sat down together, Amy was attracted to Dale, even though she barely knew who he was. She had heard of the name Earnhardt, but she had never watched a NASCAR race and knew nothing about Dale's racing career. Nevertheless, when he finally asked her out, she said yes. They started dating soon after that first meeting.

Having a steady girlfriend was a big change for Dale. Before Amy, Dale's entire world revolved around racing. He was used to staying up all night playing video games with his friends and sleeping all day long. He ate only take-out food like pizza and burgers. Amy started taking him out to nice restaurants and to museums. She taught him to keep more regular hours. And she showed him how to cook his own meals and to choose healthier foods.

As it turned out, Amy didn't just redesign Dale's house. She moved into it with him! In fact,

the two of them grew so close that Dale didn't like
to leave the house without her.

CHAPTER 7
Returning Champion

In some ways, Dale's relationship with Amy Reimann helped him become a better person. And it also seemed to help him become a better driver.

In the years between 2008 and 2014, Dale continued to win races and compete for the

Most Popular Driver
DALE EARNHARDT, JR.

NASCAR Cup. But he also lost focus and fell into long slumps. He would start out a race in the lead, then lose concentration and let another driver pass him in the last few laps. Sometimes he would go years without winning a race. He was voted Most Popular Driver every year, but he worried that he was disappointing his loyal fans.

After Amy moved in with Dale in 2011, she encouraged him to get more serious about his driving. Dale began spending more time with Steve Letarte, the new chief of his pit crew. Together, Dale and Steve sat in on the practice sessions of other successful drivers, to see what they could improve about their own performance. Dale also began to work harder on his physical fitness. He cut back on his beer drinking and started running on a treadmill regularly.

Steve Letarte

Over time, Dale's changes began to pay off. He started finishing races strong again. In 2013, he scored twenty-two top-ten finishes—a career high. He still had trouble winning races, though. At one point, he went fifty-five races without finishing in first place. But he knew he was getting closer.

Dale seemed to save his best driving for the Daytona 500. He finished second there in 2010, then again in 2012 and 2013. But he wasn't happy being the runner-up. He had won there once before, and he knew he could win there again.

2013's top three drivers from the Daytona 500:
Dale Earnhardt Jr. (2nd), Jimmie Johnson (1st), and Mark Martin (3rd)

Pit Stop

Being a great driver means having a great pit crew. During a race, the pit crew is in charge of changing tires, making repairs, and putting gas in the car. A good NASCAR pit crew can change all four tires, refuel, and get the driver back on the track again in under fifteen seconds.

NASCAR pit crews are made up of five main jobs:

- The *crew chief* is the leader of the pit crew.
- The *jack man* lifts the car up so the tires can be changed.
- The *tire carrier* carries tires to the car. The tires can weigh more than fifty pounds.
- The *tire changer* removes the old tires and puts on new ones.
- The *gas man* refuels the car.

Jack man

In 2014, Dale arrived in Daytona with one goal in mind: win the Great American Race for the first time in ten years. The only thing that held him back was bad weather. A rainstorm caused the race to be halted a fifth of the way through. When the delay began, Dale was in eighteenth place. The storm was so bad, the rain delay lasted for more than six hours. It was the longest delay in Daytona 500 history.

Dale spent that time in the clubhouse on his cell phone. Nearby, Amy and his sister Kelley played cards to pass the time. The drivers were called back to their cars around eight in the evening. The rest of this race would take place under the bright lights of the Daytona superspeedway.

Dale marched out to the track with a determined look in his eye. He knew what he had to do to come back and win the race. With seventy laps remaining, Dale surged into the lead

and never looked back. He held off Jeff Gordon
and Jimmie Johnson down the stretch to capture
his second Daytona crown.

If his first victory was sweet, this one was even sweeter. In 2004, Dale had been the young and hungry one. Now he was the beloved veteran on the comeback trail. Even better, Dale had now done something even his father could not: win the Daytona 500 twice. As he rolled into Victory Lane, Dale made sure to soak it all in. He knew he might never get back there again.

Dale after winning the Daytona 500 in 2004 and 2014

CHAPTER 8
The Finish Line

In June 2015, Dale and Amy got engaged. They were married on New Year's Eve 2016 at a North Carolina winery. Several NASCAR stars were in attendance, including Chocolate Myers, Bubba Wallace, and Danica Patrick—who caught Amy's bouquet.

A few months earlier, Dale had been involved in a minor accident that turned out to have a major effect on his career. In June 2016, while driving at the Michigan International Speedway, Dale's car lost control and hit a wall. He was forced to leave the race.

Over the next month, Dale began experiencing strange symptoms. He had trouble keeping his balance. His vision became blurry. And he had bad headaches. Dale recognized these as signs of a concussion, like the one he'd had before. He kept on racing, but made an appointment to see his doctor.

The doctor confirmed that Dale did have a concussion. But this time, it was more serious. He advised Dale to stop racing—at least temporarily, until his brain could heal. Dale took his doctor's advice and announced that he would be taking a break from NASCAR. He would not return until the next Daytona 500, in February 2017.

Even though he missed the entire second half of the NASCAR season, Dale still won the Most Popular Driver Award for the fourteenth year in a row.

Dale started therapy to heal his concussion.

His doctor gave him a series of exercises to do. They were like a workout for his brain. The physical therapy was very frustrating. Dale was used to doing everything at top speed. But he needed patience to exercise and recover properly. He felt like he should be getting better, but it was all going very slowly.

At times, Dale would find he was shaking uncontrollably. He would get dizzy just walking across a room. Many days he would wake up in a bad mood. He wondered if he would ever get back to racing. Through all his struggles, Amy stayed by his side and encouraged him to keep fighting.

By December 2016, Dale started to feel better. His doctor said that he was well enough to race again. To be on the safe side, Dale decided to take another couple of months off. He announced that he would return to the track in February, at the Daytona 500.

Daytona had always been a special place for Dale. Although he was involved in a crash and didn't finish the race, he was excited to be back on the oval where he belonged. But a part of Dale knew that his career as a driver might be coming to an end.

On April 25, 2017, Dale announced that 2017 would be his final year driving full-time. He thanked his pit crew, his racing team, and the fans of "Junior Nation" for their support.

He also thanked his father for inspiring him to become a NASCAR driver.

At the end of the year, Dale won his fifteenth consecutive Most Popular Driver Award.

He finished his career with twenty-six wins in the NASCAR Cup Series, a total that ranks him in the top forty in NASCAR history. Tributes poured in from all over, including from other drivers whom Dale had competed against.

Although Dale was done racing, he kept up a busy schedule after his retirement.

The NBC television network hired him to be a NASCAR commentator for their broadcasts. He

continued in his role as a team owner and host of numerous NASCAR radio and TV shows. He wrote a book, called *Racing to the Finish*, detailing his battle to recover from his concussion.

In May 2018, Dale and Amy welcomed their first child, Isla Rose Earnhardt, into the world. Two years later, they announced that they were expecting a second child. Nicole Lorraine Earnhardt was born in October 2020. And at that year's Daytona 500, Dale was named the Honorary Starter and waved the green flag to officially begin the race.

Just a few months later, Dale was elected to the NASCAR Hall of Fame. Accepting the honor, Dale thanked the voters for recognizing his achievements and summed up his contribution to the sport.

NASCAR Hall of Fame

"I wasn't always perfect," he said. "I didn't have the success that my father did. I gained a ton of fans because of who I was. I didn't squander that. I didn't ruin that. I grew that base and introduced the sport to a lot of people who hadn't heard of Dale Earnhardt. I always felt like the sport needed to be healthy long after my driving career was over. It's important to me that our sport survives and stays strong long after my life is over."

Timeline of Dale Earnhardt Jr.'s Life

1974 — Dale Earnhardt Jr. born October 10 in Kannapolis, North Carolina

1996 — Races in the Busch Series for the first time

1998 — Wins first Busch Series title

1999 — Makes NASCAR Cup debut

2000 — Wins first NASCAR Cup race

2001 — Dale Earnhardt Sr. dies

2002 — Appears on the cover of *NASCAR Thunder 2003* video game

2003 — Wins NASCAR's Most Popular Driver Award for the first time

2004 — Wins first Daytona 500

2006 — Appears in the film *Talladega Nights*

2007 — Announces move to Hendrick Motorsports and changes number to #88

2014 — Wins second Daytona 500

2016 — Marries Amy Reimann

2017 — Retires from driving

— Wins his fifteenth consecutive Most Popular Driver Award

2018 — First child, Isla Rose, is born

2020 — Elected to NASCAR Hall of Fame

— Second child, Nicole Lorraine, is born

Timeline of the World

1974 — Hank Aaron breaks Babe Ruth's record by hitting his 715th career home run

1976 — America celebrates its bicentennial

1980 — Mount St. Helens, a volcano in Washington State, erupts

1985 — Wreck of the RMS *Titanic* located

1989 — Animated series *The Simpsons* debuts

1990 — Hubble Space Telescope is launched

1996 — The city of Atlanta, Georgia, hosts the Summer Olympics

1998 — President Bill Clinton is impeached

2001 — September 11 terrorist attacks kill almost three thousand people in the United States

2004 — Social media network Facebook is launched

2008 — Barack Obama is elected the first Black president of the United States

2010 — Oil company BP's Deepwater Horizon oil rig explodes in the Gulf of Mexico

2013 — Black Lives Matter social justice movement begins

2017 — Category 5 storm Hurricane Maria devastates the island of Puerto Rico

2020 — The coronavirus disease COVID-19 pandemic wreaks havoc worldwide

Bibliography

*Books for young readers

Anderson, Lars. "Dale Earnhardt Jr.'s Retirement: A Love Story." *Bleacher Report*, April 28, 2017. https://bleacherreport.com/articles/2706296-dale-earnhardt-jrs-retirement-a-love-story.

Bernstein, Viv. "Father's Legacy Inspires Earnhardt Jr." *New York Times*, February 16, 2004. https://www.nytimes.com/2004/02/16/sports/auto-racing-father-s-legacy-inspires-earnhardt-jr.html.

Busbee, Jay. *Earnhardt Nation: The Full-Throttle Saga of NASCAR's First Family*. New York: HarperCollins, 2017.

Cothren, Larry, and the Editors of *Stock Car Racing Magazine*. *Dale Earnhardt Jr.: Making a Legend of His Own*. St. Paul, MN: Motorbooks, 2005.

Earnhardt, Dale, Jr. *Driver #8*. With Jade Gurss. New York: Warner Books, 2002.

Earnhardt, Dale, Jr. *Racing to the Finish: My Story*. With Ryan McGee. Nashville, TN: Thomas Nelson, 2018.

El-Bashir, Tarik. "Never on Sunday, Until Now for Earnhardt." *New York Times*, February 16, 1998. https://www.nytimes.com/1998/02/16/sports/auto-racing-never-on-sunday-until-now-for-earnhardt.html.

Hembree, Mike. *Dale Earnhardt Jr.: Out of the Shadow of Greatness*. New York: Skyhorse Publishing, 2013.

Knotts, Bob. "One Driven Family." *USA Weekend*, August 28–30, 1998.

Lemasters, Ron, Jr., and Al Pearce. *Dale Earnhardt Jr.: Inside the Rise of a NASCAR Superstar*. St. Paul, MN: Motorbooks, 2006.

*Pimm, Nancy Roe. *The Daytona 500: The Thrill and Thunder of the Great American Race*. Minneapolis, MN: Millbrook Press, 2011.